ISBN 978-1-331-37426-8
PIBN 10181086

This book is a reproduction of an important historical work. Forgotten Books uses state-of-the-art technology to digitally reconstruct the work, preserving the original format whilst repairing imperfections present in the aged copy. In rare cases, an imperfection in the original, such as a blemish or missing page, may be replicated in our edition. We do, however, repair the vast majority of imperfections successfully; any imperfections that remain are intentionally left to preserve the state of such historical works.

1 MONTH OF
FREE
READING

at
www.ForgottenBooks.com

By purchasing this book you are
eligible for one month membership to
ForgottenBooks.com, giving you
unlimited access to our entire
collection of over 700,000 titles via
our web site and mobile apps.

To claim your free month visit:
www.forgottenbooks.com/free181086

Similar Books Are Available from
www.forgottenbooks.com

MEMOIR

OF

REV. PATRICK COPLAND

RECTOR ELECT OF THE FIRST PROJECTED COLLEGE IN
THE UNITED STATES

A Chapter of the English Colonization of America

BY

EDWARD D. NEILL

AUTHOR OF "TERRA MARIÆ," THE "VIRGINIA COMPANY," THE
"ENGLISH COLONIZATION OF AMERICA DURING THE SEVENTEENTH CENTURY," ETC.

"Nec falsa dicere, nec vera reticere"

NEW YORK

CHARLES SCRIBNER & CO., 654 BROADWAY

1871

22-?
N41

PREFACE.

LIVING, as Copland did, in a period of political and ecclesiastical convulsion; indulging neither in political acerbity, nor the "odium theologicum," yet not afraid to differ from popular modes of thought and worship, to correspond with Hugh Peters, once the fiery preacher at Salem, Massachusetts, and, at the same time, to call Nicholas Ferrar, the gentle ritualistic recluse of Little Gidding, his friend, it is not strange that his name was not written in large letters by the trimming historians of the era of the vacillating Charles and determined Cromwell, who seemed to think it a work of merit, to hurl words, like barbed arrows, against all who differed from them an iota.

The establishment of Christianity in America, in Copland's day, largely occupied the attention of the Church. Sir William Alexander, Secretary of State for Scotland, and proprietor of Nova Scotia, as early as 1614, wrote, in one of his poems—

"In this last age, Time doth new worlds display,
   That Christ a Church o'er all the earth may have;
His righteousness shall barbarous realms away,
   If their first love more civil lands will leave:
America to Europe may succeed;
God may stones raise up to Abram's seed."

From year to year the enthusiasm on this subject increased. Poets and divines vied with each other in portraying a bright future for the New World. John Donne, Dean of St. Paul's, in closing his sermon before the Virginia Company, said :—

" Those among you that are old now, shall pass out of this world with this great comfort, that you contributed to the beginning of the Commonwealth and the Church, although not to see the growth thereof to perfection ; Apollos watered, but Paul planted ; he that begun the work was the greater man. And you that are young men may live to see the enemy as much impeached by that place, and your friends, yea, children, as well accommodated in that place as any other. You shall have made this *island*, which is but as the *suburbs* of the Old World, a bridge—a gallery to the New, to join all to that world that shall never grow old, the kingdom of Heaven."

George Herbert, the holy singer of the Church of England, crystallized this thought a few years later in the words—

" Religion stands tip-toe in our land,
   Ready to pass to the American strand.
   When height of malice and prodigies, lusts,
   Impudent sinning, witchcraft, and distrusts,
   The marks of future bane, shall fill our cup ;
   When Seine shall swallow Tiber, and the Thames,
   By letting in them both, pollutes her streams ;
   When Italy of us shall have her will,
   And all her calendar of sins fulfil ;
   Whereby one may foretell what sins next year
   Shall both in France and England domineer ;

Then shall Religion to America flee,
They have their time of Gospel, e'en as we."

As he drew near death, the author, placing the manuscript containing these lines in the hands of one by his bedside, said, "I pray, deliver this little book to my dear brother Ferrar." When Nicholas Ferrar applied at Cambridge for permission to publish the poem, the Vice-Chancellor at first refused to allow it to be printed unless the above verses were stricken out; but Mr. Ferrar refusing to comply, a licence to print was reluctantly granted. Two or three years later, Dr. Twisse, writing to the learned Mede, said:

"Now, I beseech you, let me know what your opinion is of our English Plantation in the New World. Heretofore, I have wondered in my thoughts at the providence of God concerning that world, not discovered till this old world of ours is almost at an end, and there no footsteps found of the knowledge of the true God, much less of Christ. And then, considering our English Plantations of late, and the opinion of many grave divines concerning the Gospel's fleeing westward, sometimes I had such thoughts—Why may not that be the place of the New Jerusalem?"

A nature as sensitive as Nicholas Ferrar's responded to every good wish for the Plantations of the Virginia Company, of which he had been the efficient Deputy-Governor, and thus became intimate with Patrick Copland, who had collected money, and requested that it should be applied to the erection of a free school in the western World. The biographer of Ferrar, speak-

PATRICK COPLAND:

AN EARLY LIGHT-BEARER TO INDIA AND AMERICA.

CHAPTER I.

SERVICE UNDER EAST INDIA COMPANY.

FOR years the merchants of London had listened to tales of the wealth "of Ormus and of Ind." As early as 1583, there were hopes entertained of a short and direct route to the renowned and far distant empire of Cathay; and one Apsley, an enterprising man, who dealt in beads, playing-cards, and gewgaws calculated to please the tastes of Orientals, told a friend that he expected to live to see a letter dated at London, on the first of May, delivered in China before midsummer, by a short passage over the American Continent, between the forty-third and forty-sixth parallel of north latitude, a thing accomplished nearly three hundred years after the enthusiastic merchant made the prediction.

In the year 1600, the leading men accustomed to assemble at the Royal Exchange, that had been dedicated to commerce by Queen Elizabeth, organized the East

India Company with the rich merchant, Thomas Smith, as Governor, and a few years after adopted as a device for their legal seal, three ostrich feathers, with "*Juvat ire per altum*" above, and encircling them, the motto, "*Tibi serviat Ultima Thule.*"

Many of the members sincerely desired that the far-off land should acknowledge Christ, and at the commencement of their trading operations, sent teachers of truth along with the cloths, looking-glasses, glittering toys, and cheap musical instruments. In their deliberations, while they exhibited an anxiety for a fair return for their outlays, in the shape of ivory, gold-dust, and choice pearls, they recognized, nevertheless, that both they and the Chinese, and Japanese, had the same " God o'er head."

An inspection of their minutes shows that they were not despisers of providence. On one occasion, the Governor of the Company proposed to relieve the poverty of some poor preachers in London, by electing three chaplains, to pray for the safe return of their fleets ; and at another period, they gravely deliberated upon the request of the Prince of Sumatra for a white wife. Two years before John Rolfe brought to England Powhatan's daughter, "of rude education, manners barbarous, and cursed generation, merely for the good and honour " of Virginia, an honourable English gentleman, in view of his child becoming an Asiatic princess, and also out of an alleged desire to propagate the Christian religion in the Pagan world, offered to give away his daughter " accomplished in music, the use of the needle, very beautiful, and of good discourse " Certain members of the Company alluding to the fact, that divines had discountenanced the yoking together of a Christian and barbarian, the anxious parent prepared an answer, showing that his willingness to present a fair daughter to a Sumatran chief was not unscriptural.[1]

As soon as the English had established a trading port at Surat, Patrick Copland, with a faith as pure, and scholarship as elevated as that of the distinguished Henry Martyn, entered the service of the East India Company as a chaplain.

During the summer of 1614, he returned to England with a talented native youth, whom he had taught chiefly by signs, " to speake, to reade and write the English tongue and hand, both Romane and Secretary, within less than the space of a yeare."[2] Soon after, he wrote to the Company that his pupil had increased in the knowledge of the Christian religion, and suggesting that he should be publicly baptized " as the first-fruits of India." Archbishop Abbott having been consulted, the Company acceded to the proposition.

An Indian, either from Hindostan or America, the Bay of Bengala or the Chesapeake, was a great rarity

---

[1] " Cal. of State Papers. East Indies, 1513—1616."
[2] " Virginia's God be Thanked." London, 1622.

in the streets of London during the reign of James the First; and as he walked, the women, with curiosity, peeped through cracks of the front doors, and children went before, and followed his steps, their mouths agape with astonishment. Shakspeare, the keen observer of the foibles of his day, alludes, in the "Tempest," to this disposition to make much of an Indian :—

"What have we here? A man or a fish? Dead or alive? A strange fish! Were I in England now, as once I was, and had but this fish painted, not a holiday fool there but would give a piece of silver. Any strange beast there makes a man; when they will not give a doit to relieve a lame beggar, they will lay out ten to see a dead Indian."

For centuries Fenchurch Street has, during Christmas week, been alive with persons busily passing to and fro; but on Sunday, 22nd of December 1616, an unusual crowd surged toward the Church of St. Dennis, for it had been announced that, by the rite of baptism, a lad, a native of Bengala, was to be initiated into the Church of Christ. The Privy Council, the Lord Mayor and Aldermen, the members of the East India, and the sister Company of Virginia, with difficulty, waded through the "sea of upturned faces" overflowing the approaches to the edifice, and the congregation within the walls was densely packed. The rite was administered by Dr. John Wood, and Petrus Papa, or Peter Pope, the name given in baptism, was chosen by King James, that odd compound of cant, coarse-

ness, and sottishness, who often seemed unable to dis-
tinguish between the odour of beer and sanctity, "the
spirit of wine and the Spirit Divine," and yet affected
to be a special "defender of the faith."

In the "Royal James," that sailed not many weeks
after the ordinance was administered, Peter Pope and
teacher departed for India. Copland was on board
during a typhoon, in which the "Unicorn," a ship of
the fleet, was wrecked upon the coast of Japan, and
he has vividly described the storm. "In this tempest we lost also our pinnace, with twenty-four or
thirty men, which we had sent before us to Firando,
an island adjoining to Japan, to give notice of our
coming, of which we never heard news. We cut off
our long-boat, and let her go; we sunk our shallop,
with two men in her, who were swallowed up by the
waves. Such was this storm, as if Jonah had been
flying into Tarshish. The air was beclouded, the
heavens were obscured, and made an Egyptian night
of five or six days perpetual horror. The experience
of our seamen was amazed; the skill of our mariners
was confounded; our 'Royal James' most violently
and dangerously leaked, and those which pumped to
keep others from drowning were half-drowned themselves."[1]

The studies of Pope were continued under the

---

[1] "Virginia's God be Thanked." Page 6.

supervision of his first teacher, and the scholar proved to be as quick-witted as the young Chinese and Japanese who are, in the nineteenth century, found in the schools of Great Britain and the United States, or engaged in trade at San Francisco and other centres of commercial transactions. Latin epistles, addressed by him, early in the year 1620, to the Governor of the East India Company, and to Martin Pring, then in command of the " Royal James," have been pre-served, which indicate not only the docility of the youth, but also how " apt to teach" was Copland.

CHAPTER II.

THE Virginia Company were the first to take steps relative to the establishment of schools in the English colonies of America. In a letter written to the authorities of the infant settlement at Jamestown, on November 18, 1618, they use these words: "Whereas, by a special grant and license from his Majesty, a general contribution over this realm hath been made for the building and planting of a college, for the training up of the children of those infidels in true religion, moral virtue, and civility, and for other godliness, we do therefore, according to a former grant and order, hereby ratify and confirm and ordain that a convenient place be chosen and set out for the planting of a university at the said Henrico in time to come, and that in the meantime preparation be there made for the building of the said college for the children of the infidels, according to such instructions as we shall deliver. And we will and ordain that ten thousand acres, partly of the land they impaled, and partly of the land within the territory of the said Henrico, be allotted and set out for the endowing of the said university and college with convenient possessions."[1]

A week after the date of this communication, a ripe scholar in England, the Rev. Thomas Lorkin, subsequently distinguished as secretary of the English embassy in France, writes to an acquaintance: "A good friend of mine proposed to me within three or four days a condition of going over to Virginia, where the Virginia Company means to erect a college, and undertakes to procure me good assurance of £200 a-year, and if I shall find any ground of dislike, liberty to return at pleasure."[2]

The offer, after due consideration, appears not to have been accepted, and nothing more was done until the reorganization of the Company in April, 1619, and the election of Sir Edwin Sandys as its presiding officer.

By his integrity, patriotism, scholarship, and great administrative talent, he infused new life into the expiring Society, and associated with him Nicholas Ferrar, the honourable merchant of London, Sir John Danvers, the step-father, and Edward Lord Cherbury, the brother of the sweet poet, George Herbert, also the Earl of Southampton, who in early life extended a helping hand to a poor boy that is said to have held horses for gentlemen at the doors of play-houses, and

[1] MSS. Virginia Records.
[2] "Court and Times of James the First, vol. ii., p. 109."

became Shakspeare, the portrayer of all the varied emotions of the soul, whose reputation as a dramatist has increased in lustre as the centuries have advanced.

The new managers of the Company proceeded to reconstruct Virginia with the most liberal views. By their permission the first representative and legislative body in America was convened at Jamestown, on July 30, 1619, in the church, the most convenient place they could find, the minister of which was Mr. Buck.

During the sessions of this body, which continued until the 4th of August, a petition was presented relative to the erection of a university and college. From this period until the dissolution of the Virginia Company, the design of a university and college was never forgotten.

The collections taken up by order of the king, for a college, in 1619 amounted to £2,043 2s. 12½d. and at a meeting of the Company on May 26th, Sir Edwin Sandys, as treasurer, propounded to the court "a thing worthy to be taken into consideration for the glory of God and honour of the Company, forasmuch as the King, in his most gracious favour, hath granted his letters to the several bishops of his kingdom for the collecting of moneys to erect and build a college in Virginia for the training and bringing up of infidels' children to the true knowledge of God and understanding of righteousness. He conceived it the fittest that as yet they should not build the college, but rather forbear awhile, and begin first with the advances they have to provide and settle an annual revenue, and out of that to begin the erection of said college. And for the performance hereof also moved that a certain piece of land be laid out at Henrico, being the place formerly resolved on, which should be called the college land, and for the planting of the same send presently fifty good persons, to be located thereon, and to occupy the same."

On June 14, 1619, it was moved by Mr. Treasurer, "that the court would take into consideration to appoint a committee of their gentlemen and other of his Majesty's counsel for Virginia concerning the college, being a weighty business, and so great that an account of their proceedings therein must be given to the State. Upon which the court, upon deliberate consideration, have recommended the rare trust unto the right worthy Sir Dudley Diggs, Sir John Danvers, Sir Nath. Rich, Sir Jo. Wolstenholme, Mr. Deputy Ferrar, Mr. Dr. Anthony, and Mr. Dr. Gulson, to meet at such time as Mr. Treasurer shall order hereto."[1]

On June the 24th the committee by the last court appointed for the college having met, as they were

---

[1] This and following extracts are from the MSS. Transactions of the London Company. The varied orthography of proper names has not been altered.

desired, delivered over their proceedings, which the court allowed, being this that followeth:

"A note of what kind of men and most fit to be sent to Virginia in the next intended voyage of transporting one hundred men.

"A minister to be entertained at the yearly allowance of forty pounds, and to have fifty acres of land for him and his for ever; to be allowed his transportation and his man's at the company's charge, and ten pounds to furnish himself withall.

"A captain thought fit, to be considered of, to take charge of such people as are to be planted on the college land.

"All the people at this first sending, except some soon to be sent as well for planting the college and public land, to be single men, unmarried.

"A warrant to be made and directed to Sir Thomas Smith for the payment of the collection money to Sir Edwin Sandys, treasurer, and that Dr. Gulstone[1] shall be entreated to present unto my Lord Primate of Canterbury such letters to be signed for the speedy paying of the moneys from every diocese which yet remain unpaid.

"The several sorts of tradesmen and others for the college land: smiths, carpenters, bricklayers, turners, potters, husbandmen, brickmakers.

[1] Gulston was a distinguished physician and founder of the Gulstonian Lectureship.

"And whereas, according to the standing order, seven were chosen by the court to be of the committee for the college, the said order allowing no more, and, inasmuch as Mr. John Wroth came in error to be left out, he is therefore now desired to be an assistant with them, and to give them meeting at such time and place as is agreed of."

At a meeting of the Company held in London, at Mr. Ferrar's house, on July 21, 1619, the Earls of Southampton and Warwick, Sir Thomas Gates, and others being present, the following anonymous letter was read :

+

I. H. S.

"SIR EDWIN SANDYS, *Treasurer of Virginia :*

"Good luck in the name of the Lord, who is daily magnified by the experiment of your zeal and piety in giving beginning to the foundation of the college in Virginia, sacred work due to Heaven and so longed for on earth.

"Now know we assuredly that the Lord will do you good and bless you in all your proceedings, even as He blessed the house of Obed Edom and all that pertaineth unto him because of the ark of God. Now that you seek the kingdom of God, all things shall be ministered unto you. This I well see already, and perceive that by your godly determination the Lord hath given you favour in the sight of all His people, and I know some whose hearts are much enlarged because of the house of the Lord our God to procure you wealth, which greater designs I have presumed to outrun with this oblation, which I humbly beseech you may be accepted as the pledge of my devotion, and as an earnest of the power which I have vowed unto the Almighty God of Jacob concerning this thing, which till I may in part perform I desire to remain unknown and unsought after.

"The things are these: a communion cup with the ewer and vase; a trencher plate for the bread; a carpet of crimson velvet; a linen damask cloth."

On Wednesday, November 17, 1619, at a great and general quarterly meeting of the Virginia Company, the treasurer referred to the instructions sent out by the new governor of the colony, Sir George Yeardley, by which were to be selected ten thousand acres of land for the university to be planted at Henrico, of which one thousand was reserved for the college for the conversion of infidels.

On December 1st, "It was propounded that in consideration of some public gifts given by sundry persons to Virginia, divers presents of church plate and other ornaments, two hundred pounds already given toward building a church, and five hundred pounds promised by another toward the educating of infidels' children, that, for the honour of God, and memorial of such good benefactors, a tablet might hang in the court with their names and gifts inserted, and the ministers of Virginia and the Sommer islands may have intelligence thereof, that for their pious works they may recommend them to God in their prayers; which generally was thought very fit and expedient."

On February 2, 1619-20—"A letter from an unknown person was read, directed to the treasurer, promising five hundred pounds for the educating and bringing up infidels' children in Christianity, which Mr. Treasurer, not willing to meddle therewith alone, desired the court to appoint a select committee for the managing and employing of it to the best purpose. They made choice of: Lord Pagett, Sir Tho. Wroth, Mr. J. Wroth, Mr. Deputie, Mr. Tho. Gibbs, Dr. Winstone, Mr. Bamfourde, and Mr. Keightley.

The Copy of the Letter.

"SIR,—Your charitable endeavour for Virginia hath made you a father, me a favourer of those good works which, although heretofore hath come near to their birth, yet for want of strength could never be delivered, (envy and division dashing these younglings even in the womb,) until your helpful hand, with other favourable personages, gave them both birth and being, for the better cherishing of which good and pious work, seeing many casting gifts into the treasury, I am encouraged to tender my poor mite; and although I cannot with the princes of Issaker bring gold and silver covering, yet offer you what I can, some goats' hair, necessary stuff for the Lord's tabernacle, protesting here in my sincerity, without Papistical merit or Pharisaical applause, wishing from my heart as much unity in your honourable undertaking as there is sincerity in my designs, to the furtherance of which good work, the converting of infidels to the faith of Christ, I promised by my good friends £500 for the maintenance of a convenient number of young Indians taken at the age of seven years, or younger, and instructed in the reading and understanding the principles of Christian Religion unto the age of twelve years, and then as occasion serveth, to be trained and brought up in some lawful trade with all humanity and gentleness until the age of one and twenty years, and then to enjoy like liberties and privileges with our native English in that place.

"And for the better performance thereof you shall receive £50 more, which shall be delivered into the hands of two religious persons with certitude of payment, who shall once every quarter examine and certify to the treasurer here, in England, the due operation of these promises, together with the names of those children just taken, the foster-fathers and overseers, not doubting but you are all assured that gifts devoted to God's service cannot be diverted to private and secular advantages without sacrilege. If your graver judgments can devise a more charitable course for the younger, I beseech you inform my friend, with your security for true performance, and my benevolence shall be always ready to be delivered accordingly.

"The greatest courtesy I expect or crave is to conceal my friend's name, lest importunity might urge him to betray that trust of secresy, which he hath faithfully promised, who hath moved my heart to this good work. I rest, *ab famo*,

" DUST AND ASHES.

" SIR EDWIN SANDYS,

" *The faithful Treasurer for Virginia.*"

On the 16th of February the following was passed :—

"Whereas, at the last court a special committee was appointed for the managing of the £500 given by an unknown person for educating the infidels' children, Mr. Treasurer signified that they have met and taken into consideration the proposition of Sir John Wolstenholme, that John Peirce and his associates might have the training and bringing up of some of these children; but the said committee, for divers reasons, think it inconvenient, first, because they intend not to go this two or three months, and then after their arrival will be long in settling themselves; as also that the Indians are not acquainted with them, and so they may stay four or five years before they have account that any good is done.[1]

"And for to put it into the hands of private men to bring them up, as was by some proposed, they thought it was not so fit, by reason of the difficulty unto which it is subject.

"But forasmuch as divers hundreds and particular plantations are already there settled, and the Indians well acquainted with them, as namely, Smith's Hundred, Martin's Hundred, Bartlett's Hundred, and the like, that, therefore, they receive and take charge of them, by which course they shall be sure to be well nurtured and have their due so long as these plantations shall hold ; and for such of the children as they find capable of learning shall be put in the college and brought up to be Fellows, and such as are not shall be put to trades and be brought up in the fear of God and the Christian religion.

"And being demanded how and by what lawful means they would preserve them, and after keep them, that they run not to join their parents or friends, and their parents or friends steal them not away, which natural affection may inforce in the one and the other, it was answered and well allowed that a treaty and

---

[1] The associates of John Peirce were William Brewster and the so-called " Pilgrim Fathers," whose landing at Plymouth Rock, Dec. 11, 1620, O.S., is the subject of a poem by Mrs. Hemans.

agreement be made with the King of that country concerning them, which if it so fall out at any time, as is expressed, they may by his command be returned.

"Whereupon Sir Thomas Roe promised that Bartlett's Hundred should take two or three, and Mr. Smith to be respondent to the Company, and because every hundred may the better consider thereof they were licensed till Sunday in the afternoon, at which time they sit at Mr. Treasurer's to bring in their answer how many they will have, and bring those that will be respondent for them, and those that others will not take Mr. Treasurer, in behalf of Smith's Hundred, hath promised to take into their charge."

"The Treasurer signified, on February 22nd, that the corporation of Smith's Hundred very well accepted of the charge of infidels' children recommended unto them by the court, in regard of their good disposition to do good; but, otherwise, if the court shall please to take it from them they will willingly give £100. And for their resolutions, although they have not yet set them down in writing, by reason of some things yet to be considered of, they will, so soon as may be, prepare the same and present it."

A box standing upon the table with this direction, "*To Sir Edwin Sandis, the faithful Treasurer for Virginia,*" he acquainted them that it was brought unto him by a man of good fashion, who would neither tell him his name nor from whence it came; but, by the subscription being the same as the letter, he considered that it might be the £550 promised them.

And it being agreed that the box should be opened, there was a bag of new gold containing the said sum of £550.

Whereupon Doctor Winstone reporting that the committee had requested for the managing thereof, and that it should be wholly in charge of Smith's Hundred; it was desired by some that the resolution should be presented in writing at the next court, which, in regard of the Ash-Wednesday sermon, was agreed to be upon Thursday afternoon.

At a meeting held at the house of Sir Edwin Sandys, on April 9, 1620, intelligence was given that Mr. Nicholas Ferrar, elder, being translated from this life[1] unto a better, had by his will bequeathed £300 towards the converting of infidels' children in Virginia,

[1] Nicholas Ferrar, Sr., was a rich merchant that had taken an interest in the voyages of Raleigh and Gilbert. After the election, in 1619, of Sir Edwin Sandys to the Governorship of Virginia Company, the meetings were held in the parlours of his capacious house in St. Sythe's Lane. He married Mary Wodenoth; and Arthur Wodenoth, who wrote a brief sketch of the Virginia Company, which was published in 1651, was probably a nephew or brother-in-law.

His son, John Ferrar, was Deputy-Governor of Virginia Company, from 1619, for two years, and after he declined re-election, his brother Nicholas was appointed, and held the office until the Company was dissolved in 1624, and in 1626 the latter was ordained in the Church of England, and retired, with

to be paid unto Sir Edwin Sandys and Mr. Jo. Ferrar, at such time as, upon certificate from there, ten of the said infidels' children shall be placed in the college, to be there disposed of by the said Sir Edwin Sandys and Jo. Ferrar, according to the true intent of the said will; and that in the mean [time] till that was performed he hath tied his executors to pay eight per cent. for the same unto three several honest men in Virginia, (such as the said Sir Edwin Sandys and John Ferrar shall approve of,) of good life and fame, that will undertake each of them to bring up one of the said children in the grounds of Christian religion, that is to say, £8 yearly apiece.

About this period Mr. George Thorpe, a gentleman of sterling character, of his Majesty's privy chamber, and one of his council for Virginia, sailed for the colony, having been appointed by the Company deputy to take charge of the college lands.

At a meeting of the Company on November 15, 1620, as the reading of the minutes of the previous meeting

his aged mother, to Little Gidding. William, another son, appears to have gone to Virginia.

John Ferrar had a talented daughter, christened Virginia. She wrote a treatise on silk-worms, and also published in 1651,

" A Mapp of Virginia discovered to ye Hills, and its latt. from 35 deg. and ½ neer Florida, to 41 deg. bounds of New England.

" Domina Virginia Farrar, Collegit.

" And sold by J. Stephenson, at ye Sunne, below Ludgate, 1651."

John Ferrar died in 1657; his daughter in 1687.

were completed, "a stranger stepped in," and presented a map of Sir Walter Raleigh's, containing a description of Guiana, and with the same four great books, as the gift of one that desired his name might not be known. One of these was a translation of St. Augustine's *City of God;* the others were the works of the distinguished Calvinist and Puritan, Mr. Perkins, "which books the donor desired might be sent to the college in Virginia, there to remain in safety to the use of the collegiate educators, and not suffered at any time to be lent abroad."

For which so worthy a gift my lord of Southampton desired the party that presented them to return deserved thanks from himself and the rest of the Company to him that had so kindly bestowed them.

The next year the interest of the Company in establishing schools in America was increased by another unexpected donation.

Mr. Copland returning home from India in 1621, met some ships on the way to Virginia, and learning the destitution of the New World colony in churches and schools, he longed to do them good. The mode devised for helping them is fully explained in the minutes of the Virginia Company.

At a court held 24th October 1621, Mr. Deputy acquainted the court "that one Mr. Copland, a minister lately returned from the East Indies, out of an earnest desire to give some furtherance unto the plantation in Virginia, had been pleased, as well by his own good example as by persuasion, to stir up many that came with him in the ship called the 'Royal James' to contribute toward some good work to be begun in Virginia, insomuch that he had already procured a matter of some £70 to be employed that way, and had also written from Cape Bona Speranza to divers parties in the East Indies to move them to some charitable contribution thereunto. So, as he hoped, they would see very shortly his letters would produce some good effect among them, especially if they might understand in what manner they intended to employ the same. It was therefore ordered that a committee should be appointed to treat with Mr. Copland about it. And forasmuch as he had so well deserved of the Company by his extraordinary care and pains in this business, it was thought fit and ordered that he should be admitted a free brother of this Company, and at the next quarter court it should be moved that some proportion of land might be bestowed upon him in gratification of his worthy endeavours to advance this extended work; and further, it was thought fit also to add thereunto a number of some other special benefactors unto the plantation whose memorial is preserved. The committee to treat with him are these: Mr. Deputy, Mr. Gibbs, Mr. Nicholas Ferrar, Mr. Bamforde, Mr. Abra. Chamberlyne, Mr. Roberts, Mr. Ayres."

On the last of October, 1621, Mr. Deputy signified that, "forasmuch as it was reserved unto the Company to determine whether the said money should be employed towards the building of a church or a school, as aforesaid, your committee appointed have had conference with Mr. Copland about it, and do hold it fit, for many important reasons, to employ the said contribution towards the erection of a public free school in Virginia, towards which an unknown person hath likewise given £30, as may appear by the report of said committee, now presented to be read.

"At a meeting of the committee on Tuesday, the 30th of October, 1621, present Mr. Deputy, Mr. Gibbs, Mr. Wroth, Mr. Ayres, Mr. Nicholas Ferrar, Mr. Roberts.

"The said committee meeting this afternoon to treat with Mr. Copland touching the dispose of the money given by some of the East India Company that came with him in the 'Royal James,' to be bestowed upon some good work for the benefit of the plantation in Virginia, the said Mr. Copland did deliver in a note the names of those that had freely and willingly contributed their moneys hereunto, which money Mr. Copland said they desired might be employed towards the building either of a church or school in Virginia, which the company should think fit. And that although the sum of money was but a small propor-

tion to perform so great a work, yet Mr. Copland
said he doubted not but to persuade the East India
Company, whom he meant to solicit, to make some
addition thereunto ; besides, he said that he had very
effectually wrote (the copy of which letter he delivered
and was read) to divers factories in the East Indies
to stir them up to the like contribution towards the
performance of this pious work, as they had already
done for a church at Wapping, to which, by his
report, they have given about £400.

"It being, therefore, now taken into consideration
whether a church or a school was most necessary, and
might nearest agree to the intentions of the donors, it
was considered that forasmuch as each particular
plantation, as well as the general, either had or ought
to have a church appropriated unto them, there was
therefore a greater want of a school than of churches.

"As also for that it was impossible, with so small
a proportion, to compass so great a work as the
building of a church would require, they therefore
conceived it most fit to resolve for the erecting of a
public free school, which, being for the education of
children and grounding them in the principles of
religion, civility of life, and human learning, seemed
to carry with it the greatest weight and highest con-
sequence unto the plantations, as that whereof both
church and commonwealth take their original foundation and happy estate, this being also so like to prove

a work most acceptable unto the planters, through want whereof they have been hitherto constrained to send their children from thence hither to be taught.

"*Secondly*—It was thought fit that the school should be placed in one of the four cities, and they conceived that Charles City, of the four, did afford the most convenient place for that purpose, as well in respect it matcheth with the best in wholesomeness of air, as also for the commodious situation thereof, being not far distant fron Henrico and other particular plantations.

"It was also thought fit that, in honour of the East India benefactors, the same should be called the East India School, who shall have precedence before any other to present their children there, to be brought up in the rudiments of learning.

"It was also thought fit that this, as a collegiate or free school, should have dependence upon the college in Virginia, which should be made capable to receive scholars from the school into such scholarships; and fellowships of said college shall be endowed withal for the advancement of scholars as they arise by degree and desert in learning.

"That, for the better maintenance of the schoolmaster and usher intended there to be placed, it was thought fit that it should be moved at the next quarter court that one thousand acres of land should be allotted unto the said school, and that tenants, besides an overseer of them, should be forthwith sent upon this charge, in the condition of apprentices, to manure and cultivate said land; and that, over and above this allowance of land and tenants to the schoolmaster, such as send their children to the school should give some benevolence unto the schoolmaster, for the better increase of his maintenance.

"That it should be specially recommended to the governor to take care that the planters there be stirred up to put their helping hands towards the speedy building of the said school, in respect that their children are likely to receive the greatest benefit thereby, in their education; and to let them know that those that exceed others in their bounty and assistance hereunto shall be privileged with the preferment of their children to these said schools before others that shall be found less worthy.

" It is likewise thought fit that a good schoolmaster be provided, forthwith to be sent unto this school.

" It was also informed, by a gentleman of this committee, that he knew one, that desired not to be named, that would bestow £30, to be added to the former sum of £70 to make it an £100 towards the building of the said school."

This report, being read, was well approved of, and thought fit to be referred for confirmation to the next quarter court. On November 19, 1621, the Company again considered the matter.

" Whereas the committee appointed to treat with

Mr. Copland about the building of the East India church, or school, in Virginia, towards which a contribution of £70 was freely given by some of the East India Company that came home in the 'Royal James,' did now make report what special reasons moved them to resolve for the bestowing of that money towards the erection of a school, rather than a church, which report is at large set down at a court held last October.

" And further, that they had allowed one thousand acres of land and five apprentices, besides an overseer, to manure, besides that benevolence that is hoped will be given by each man that sends his children thither to be taught, for the schoolmaster's maintenance in his first beginning; which allowance of land and tenants, being put to the question, was well approved of, and referred for confirmation to the quarter court; provided that in the establishment hereof the Company reserve unto themselves power to make laws and orders for the better government of the said school and the revenues and profits that shall thereunto belong.

" It was further moved that, in respect of Mr. Copland, minister, hath been a chief cause of procuring this former contribution to be given by the aforesaid Company, and had also writ divers letters to many factories in the East Indies to move them to follow this good example, for the better advancement of this pious work, that therefore the Company would please to gratify him with some proportion of land.

"Whereupon the court, taking it into consideration, and being also informed that Mr. Copland was furnishing out persons to be transported this present voyage to plant and inhabit upon said lands as should be granted unto them by the Company, they were the rather induced to bestow upon him an extraordinary gratification of three shares of land, old adventure, which is three hundred acres, upon a first division, without paying rent to the Company, referring the further ratification of the said gift to the quarter court, as also his admittance of being a free brother of this Company."

About this time a young Puritan minister, John Brinsley, a nephew of the so-called English Seneca, the distinguished Bishop Hall, and the private secretary of his uncle at the synod of Dort, who also in after life became the author of many classical and theological treatises, prepared a little book suitable for the projected school in Virginia. As published, it made a small quarto of eighty-four pages, and was a plea for learning and the schoolmaster. He stated that the incivility "amongst maniè of the Irish, the Virgineans, and all other barbarous nations," grew "from their exceeding ignorance of our holy God and of all true and good learning." On another page he adds that it was his unfeigned desire to adapt the book "for all functions and places, and more particularly to every ruder place, as to the ignorant country of Wales, and more especially to that poor Irish nation, with our loving countrymen of Virginia." [1]

At a court held for Virginia the 19th of December 1621, Mr. Balmfield signified unto the court of a book

[1] In the library of University of Dublin is a copy of this work, prepared especially for the Virginia Company's plantations, with the following title—

A

CONSOLATION
For our Grammar
SCHOOLES or a faithful and most comfortable in-
couragement for laying of a sure foundation
of a good learninge in our Schooles
and for prosperous building thereunto;
More *specially for all those of the inferiour*
sort and all
rude countries and places, namely,
for *Ireland, Wales, Virginia,* with the *Sommer
Ilands*
and for the more speedie attaining of our
English tongue by the same labour, that all
speake one and the same
language:
And withall for the helping of all such as are de-
sirous speedlie to recover that which they had formerlie
got in the Grammar Schooles and to proceed aright
therein for the perpetual benefit of these our
Nations, and of the churches
of Christ.
London: Printed by Richard Field, for Thomas Man,
dwelling in Paternoster Row, at the sign
of the Talbot: 1622

" compiled by a painful schoolmaster, one Mr. John
Brinsley ;" whereupon the court gave order that the
Company's thanks should be given unto him, and
appointed a select committee to peruse the said book,
viz.—Sir John Danvers, Mr. Deputy, Mr. Gibbs, Mr.
Wroth, Mr. Balmfield, Mr. Copland, Mr. Ayres, and
Mr. Nicho. Ferrar, who are entreated to meet when
Mr. Deputy shall appoint, and after to make report of
their opinions touching the same at the next court.

At a court held for Virginia, on Wednesday, the
16th January, 1621, [1622,] the committee appointed
to peruse the book which Mr. John Brinsley, schoolmaster, presented at the last court, touching the
education of the younger sort of scholars, forasmuch
as they had as yet no time to peruse the same, by
reason of many businesses that did arise, they desired
of the court some longer respite, which was granted
unto them.   Mr. Copland, being present, was entreated to peruse it in the meantime, and deliver his
opinion thereof to the committee, at their meeting,
about it.[1]

At a quarter court held on January 30, 1621-2,
"the letter subscribed D. and A., brought to the
former court by an unknown messenger, was now

---

[1] Brinsley in an epistle addresses the Virginian Company concerning his book, as follows :—

"The triall whereof I dare (through God's goodnesse) tender to
any by yourselues appointed to make full demonstration of it,

again presented to be read, the contents whereof are as follows :—

"'January 28, 1621.

"'Most Worthy Company,—Whereas I sent the Treasurer and yourselves a letter, subscribed 'Dust

to their like, as I haue formerly done to the most learned and fit that I could chuse to this purpose, as appeareth in the Examiner's Censure in the closing of this little Treatise. And withal to help that we may haue by the same not only the puritie of our owne language preserued amongst all our own people there, but also that it may be readily learned in the Schooles, together with the Latin and other tongues, and so more propagated to the rudest Welch and Irish.

"Thus have I presumed to tender vnto you (right Honourable and right Worshipfull) whatsoe the Lord hath vouchsafed me, whereof I haue had hope that it might help you in your gouernment and charges for the good of those poore people committed to you, and specially which might further the happy successe of that so much desired plantation . . . which, if after further triall made by you, it shall be as curteously accepted as it is heartily and cheerefully offered according to that which I haue receiued from the Lord, I shall haue not only some cause to blesse His heavenly Maiesty, but also be encouraged still to prosecute these poore trauels, and to study the further good of them all during life, especially for drawing the poor natiues in Virginia, and all other of the rest of the rude and barbarous from Sathan to God, and so rest

"Yours in all humble observance
and hearty prayer to God for you,

"John Brinsley."

The Examiners to whom he alludes were "James Ussher, Doctour and Professor of Divinitie in Universitie of Dublin; Daniel Featly, Doctour of Divinitie, and Chaplin in house to his Grace of Canterburie," who wrote their commendation March 15, 1620-21

and Ashes,' which promised £550, and did, some
time afterward, according to my promise, send the
said money to Sir Edwin Sandys, to be delivered to
the Company. In which letter I did not directly
order the bestowing of the said money, but showed
my interest for the conversion of infidels' children, as
it will appear by that letter, which I desire may be
read in open court, wherein I chiefly commended the
ordering thereof to the wisdom of the honourable
Company. And whereas the gentlemen of Southampton Hundred have undertaken the disposing of
the said £550, I have long attended to see the erecting of some schools, or other way whereby some of
the children of the Virginians might have been taught
and brought up in the Christian religion and good
manners, which are not being done according to my
intent, but the money detained by a private Hundred
all this while, contrary to my mind, though I judge
very charitably of that honourable Society. And as
already you have received a great and the most pain-
fully gained part of my estate towards the laying of
the foundation of the Christian religion, and helping
forward of this pious work in that heathen, now
Christian, land, so now I require of the whole body
of the honourable and worthy Company, whom I
entrusted with the disposal of said moneys, to see the
same speedily and faithfully converted to the work
intended. And I do further propound to your honour-

able Company, that if you will procure that some of the male children of the Virginians, though but a few, be brought over into England here to be educated and taught, and to wear a habit as the children of Christ's Hospital do, and that you will be pleased to see the £550 converted to this use, then I faithfully promise to add £450 more, to make the sum £1,000, which, if God permit, I will cheerfully send you, only I desire to nominate the first tutor or governor who shall take charge to nurse and instruct them. But if you, in your wisdom, like not this motion, then my humble suit unto the whole body of your honourable Company is that my former gift of £550 be wholly employed and bestowed upon a free school to be erected in Southampton Hundred, so it be presently employed, or such other place as I or my friends shall well like, wherein both English and Virginians may be taught together, and that the said school be endowed with such privileges as you, in your wisdom, shall think fit. The master of which school, I humbly crave, may not be allowed to go over except he first bring to the Company sound testimony of his sufficiency in learning and sincerity of life.

"'The Lord give you wise and understanding hearts, that his work therein be not negligently performed. "'D. AND A.

"'*The Right Honourable and Worthy the*
"'Treasurer, Council and Company of Virginia.'"

The letter being referred to the consideration of this court, forasmuch as it did require an account of this Company how they have expended the said money, viz., the £550 in gold for the bringing up of the infidels' children in true religion and Christianity, Sir Edwin Sandys declared that the said money coming unto him enclosed in a box in the time of his being treasurer, not long after a letter subscribed "Dust and Ashes" had been directed unto him in the quality of treasurer, and delivered in the court and there openly read. He brought the money also to the next court in the box unopened, whereupon the court, after a large and serious deliberation how the said money might be best employed to the use intended, at length resolved that it was fittest to be entertained by the Societies of Southampton Hundred and Martin's Hundred, and easy to undertake for a certain number of infidels' children to be brought up by them and amongst them in Christian religion, and some good trade to live by according to the donor's religious desire.

But Martin's Hundred desired to be excused by reason their plantation was sorely weakened and then in much confusion; wherefore it being pressed that Southampton Hundred should undertake the whole, they also considering, together with the weight, the difficulty also and hazard of the business, were likewise very unwilling to undertake the managing thereof, and offered an addition of £100 more unto the former sum of £550, that it might not be put upon them.

But being earnestly pressed thereunto by the court, and finding no other means how to set forward that great work, yielded in fine to accept thereof.

Whereupon, soon after, at an assembly of that Society, the adventurers entered into a careful consideration how this great and mighty business might, with the most speed and great advantage, be effected.

Whereupon it was agreed and reported by them to employ the said money, together with an addition out of the Society's purse of a far greater sum, toward the furnishing out of Captain Bluett and his companions, being so very able and sufficient workmen, with all manner of provisions for the setting up of an iron work in Virginia, whereof the profits arising were intended and ordered in a rateable proportion to be faithfully employed for the educating of thirty of the infidels' children in Christian religion, and otherwise as the donor had required.

To which end they writ very effectual letters unto Sir George Yeardley, then governor of Virginia, and captain also of Southampton plantation, not only commending the excellence of the work, but also furnishing him at large with advice and direction how to proceed therein, with a most earnest adjuration, and that often iterated in all their succeeding letters, so to employ his best care and industry therein, as a work wherein the eyes of God, angels, and men were fixed. The copy of my letter and direction, through some omission of their officer, was not entered in their book, but a course should be taken to have it recovered.

In answer of this letter they received a letter from Sir George Yeardley, showing how difficult a thing it was at that time to obtain any of their children with the consent and good liking of their parents, by reason of their tenderness of them, or fear of hard usage by the English, unless it might be by a treaty with Opachankano, the King, which treaty was appointed to be that summer, wherein he would not fail to do his uttermost endeavours.

But Captain Bluett dying shortly after his arrival, it was a great setting back of the iron work intended; yet since that time there had been orders to restore that business with a fresh supply, so as he hoped will the gentleman that gave this gift should receive good satisfaction by the faithful account which they should be able and at all times would be ready to give, touching the employment of the said money.

Concerning which Sir Edwin Sandys further said that, as he could not but highly commend the gentleman for his worthy and most Christian act, so he had observed so great inconvenience by his modesty and eschewing of show of vain glory by concealing his name, whereby they were deprived of the mutual help and advice which they might have had by conferring with him; and whereby also he might have received more clear satisfaction with what integrity, care, and industry they had managed that business, the success whereof must be submitted to the pleasure of God, as it had been commended to His blessing.

He concluded that if the gentleman would either vouchsafe himself or send any of his friends to confer with the said Society, they would be glad to apply themselves to give him all good satisfaction. But for his own particular judgment he doubted that neither of the two courses particularized in this last letter, now read in court, would attain the effect so much desired. Now, to send for them into England and to have them educated here, he found, upon experience of those brought by Sir Tho. Dale, might be far from the Christian work intended. Again, to begin with building of a free school for them in Virginia, he doubted, considering that none of the buildings they there intended had yet prospered, by reason that as yet, through their doting so much upon tobacco, no fit workman could be had but at intolerable rates, it might rather tend to the exhausting of this sacred treasure in some small fabric, than to accomplish such a foundation as might satisfy men's expectations.

Whereupon, he wished again some meeting between the gentleman or his friends and Southampton Society, that all things being debated at full, and judiciously weighed, some constant course might be resolved on, and pursued for proceeding in and perfecting of this most pious work, for which he prayed the blessing of God to be upon the author thereof; and all the company said Amen.

In the midst of this narration a stranger stepped in, presenting four books fairly bound, sent from a person refusing to be named, who had bestowed them upon the college in Virginia, being from the same man that gave heretofore four other great books; the names of those he now sent were, viz.—a large Church Bible, the Common Prayer Book, Ursinus's Catechism, and a small Bible richly embroidered.

The court desired the messenger to return the gentleman that gave them, general acknowledgment of much respect and thanks due unto him.

A letter was also presented from one that desired not as yet to be named, with £25 in gold, to be employed by way of addition to the former contribution towards the building of a free school in Virginia, to make the other sum £125, for which the Company desired the messenger to return him their hearty thanks.

Mr. Copland moved that, whereas it was ordered by the last quarter court that an usher should be sent to Virginia, with the first convenience, to instruct the children in the free school there intended to be erected, that forasmuch as there was now a very good scholar whom he well knew, and had good testimony for his sufficiency in learning and good carriage, who offered himself to go for the performance of this service, he therefore thought good to acquaint the court therewith, and to leave it to their better judgment and consideration, whereupon the court appointed a committee, to treat with the said party, viz., Mr. Gibbs, Mr. Wroth, Mr. Wrote, Mr. Copland, Mr. Balmford, Mr. Roberts, who are to join herein with the rest of the committee and to meet about it upon Monday next, in the morning about eight, at Mr. Deputy's, and hereof to make report.

On February 27, 1621-2, the committee's report touching the allowance granted unto the usher of the free school intended in Virginia being read, Mr. Copland signified that the said usher having lately imparted his mind unto him, seemed unwilling to go as usher or any less title than master of the said school, and also to be assured of that allowance that is intended to be appropriated to the master for his proper maintenance.

But it was answered that they might not swerve from the order of the quarter court, which did appoint the usher to be first established, for the better advancement of which action divers had underwritten to a roll for that purpose drawn, which did already arise to a good sum of money, and was like daily to increase by reason of men's affections to forward so good a

work.   In which respect many sufficient scholars did
now offer themselves to go upon the same condition
as had been proposed to this party, yet in favour of
him, forsomuch as he was specially recommended by
Mr. Copland, whom the Company do much respect,
the court is pleased to give him some time to consider
of it between this and the next court, desiring then
to know his direct answer, whether he will accept of
the place of usher as has been offered unto him.   And
if he shall accept thereof, then the court have entreated
Mr. Balmford, Mr. Copland, Mr. Caswell, Mr. Mollinge,
to confer with him about the method of teaching, and
the books he intends to instruct children by.

On the 13th of March the court, taking into
their consideration certain propositions presented unto
them by Mr. Copland in behalf of Mr. Dike, formerly
commended for the usher's place in the free school
intended at Charles city, in Virginia, they have agreed
in effect unto his several requests, namely, that upon
certificates from the governor of Virginia, of his
sufficiency and diligence in training up of youth committed to his charge, he shall be confirmed in the
place of the master of the said school.

Secondly, that if he can procure an expert writer to
go over with him that can withal teach the grounds
of arithmetic whereby to instruct the children in
matters of account, the Company are contented to
give such a one his passage, whose pains they doubt

not will well be rewarded by those whose children shall be taught by him.

And for the allowance of one hundred acres of land he desires for his own proper inheritance, it is agreed that after he had served out his time, which is to be five years at least, and longer during his own pleasure, he giving a year's warning upon his remove, whereby another may be provided in his room, the Company are pleased to grant him one hundred acres.

It is also agreed that he shall be furnished with books, first for the school, for which he is to be accountable; and for the children the Company have likewise undertaken to provide good store of books, fitting for their use, for which their parents are to be answerable.

Lastly, it is ordered that the agreement between him and the Company shall, according to his own request, be set down in writing, by way of articles indented.

Upon the same day the following minute was entered on the journal of the Company :—

" Whereas, Mr. Deputy acquainted the former court with that news he had received by word of mouth, of the safe arrival of eight of their ships in Virginia, with all their people and provisions sent out this last summer, he now signified that the general letter has come to his hands, imparting as much as had been formerly delivered, which letter for more particular

D

relations did refer to the letters sent by the 'George,' which he hoped they should shortly hear of.

" Upon declaration of the Company's thankfulness unto God for the joyful and welcome news from Virginia, a motion was made that this acknowledgment of their thankfulness might not only be done in a private court, but published by some learned minister in a sermon to that purpose, before a general assembly of the Company, which motion was well approved of and thought fit to be taken into consideration upon return of the 'George,' which was daily expected, when they hoped they should receive more particular advertisement concerning their affairs in Virginia."

Early in. April 1622, the following action was taken :—

" Forasmuch as the ' George' was now safe returned from Virginia, confirming the good news they had formerly received of the safe arrival of their ships and people in Virginia, sent this last time, it was now thought fit and resolved according to a motion formerly made to the like effect, that a sermon should be preached to express the Company's thankfulness unto God for this His great and extraordinary blessing.

"To which end the court entreated Mr. Copland, being present, to take the pains to preach the said sermon, being a brother of the Company, and one that was well acquainted with the happy success of their affairs in Virginia this last year.

"Upon which request, Mr. Copland was pleased to undertake it, and therefore two places being proposed where this exercise should be performed, namely, St. Michael's in Cornhill or Bowe Church, it was by erection of hands appointed to be in Bowe Church, on Wednesday next, being the 17th day of this present month of April, about 4 o'clock in the afternoon, for which purpose Mr. Carter is appointed to give notice of the time and place to all the Company."

CHAPTER III.

COPLAND'S SERMON AT BOW CHURCH.

AFTER the great fire in London, Bow Church was altered and renovated by the celebrated architect, Sir Christopher Wren; but in 1622 it was a venerable time-stained pile, erected in the days of William the Conqueror, and the first in the city built on arches of stone, and hence called St. Marie de arcubus, then St. Mary-le-bow, and at length abbreviated by the busy Londoners into Bow Church. For more than a century the curfew, from its belfry, had been familiar to the citizens, and as it rung at nine o'clock, every apprentice tore himself away from the maiden he loved, or boon companions, and hurried home, fearing, if he was too late, that his unsympathizing master would meet him with a frown.

On Thursday, the 18th of April,[1] about four of the clock in the afternoon, the ringing of Bow Bell signified that there was to be a special service. The wealthy merchants of Lombard Street left the counting-rooms,

[1] The time of delivery was changed from Wednesday to Thursday.

and handsomely-dressed women, from the fashionable residences on St. Sythe's Lane, slowly moved, in sedans, toward this central church, to listen to the Thanksgiving sermon ordered by the Virginia Company, about to be preached by the eloquent and enthusiastic Copland. The text selected was most appropriate, consisting of that portion of the 107th Psalm from the twenty-second verse, describing the actions and feelings of sailors in a violent storm, and their joy at reaching a quiet haven.

He commenced by stating that the occasion of their assembling was to celebrate the goodness of God, and to give public thanks for the arrival of the fleet of nine ships in Virginia, during the last November and December, and the safe landing of eight hundred men, women, and children. In unfolding the text, he spoke of their dangers, deliverance, and consequent duty. In alluding to the dangers of mariners, his sentences were graphic :—

" It is next to famine, imprisonment, and a deadly disease to be a seaman; for as one saith, ' *Navigantes neque inter vivos neque inter mortuos*,' sailors are neither amongst the living, nor yet amongst the dead, as, having but a few inches of plank between them and death, they hang between both, ready to offer up their souls to every flaw of wind and billow of water wherein they are tossed. The immoveable rocks, and the

mutable winds; the overflowing waters and swallow-
ing sands; the tempestuous storms and spoiling pirates,
have their lives at their mercy and command. Mariners, living in the sea almost, as fishes, having the
waters as their necessariest element, are commonly
men void of fear, venturous, and contemners of
dangers; yet when God, on a sudden, commandeth a
storm, and sitteth Himself in the mouth of the tempest,
when their ship is foundrèd with water under them;
when life and soul are ready to shake hands and
depart this present world, then, even these nought-
fearing fellows, these high-stomaked men, tremble for
fear, like faint-hearted women, that shrink at every
stir in a wherry on the River of Thames, in a rough
and boisterous tide, or like unto a young soldier,
which starteth at the shooting off of a gun."

After he spoke of the dangers of mariners, he
continued :—

"But you will say, what needeth all this discourse
touching the danger of sea-men : we are met together
for another purpose — to giue thanks vnto God ?
Beloved, I doe confesse, indeed it is so, that the end
of our present meeting is for Thankesgiuing. But
how can we euer be feelingly thankfull as we should,
in word and deed, if wee know not the danger wherein
wee are, and the deliuerance vouchsafed vnto us?

Will not the true knowledge and deepe consideration of these make vs put so many the more thankes vnto our sacrifice of prayse?

"Wherefore, I beseech you to take to heart—*First,* the danger of your people in their passages both to Virginia and after their landing. *Secondly,* the danger of your whole colony there. *Thirdly,* the danger of yourselues here at home. And lest others that are not of your Honourable Company may thinke this point impertinent to them, let all of us consider the dangers wherein we are, and still are, and the many deliuerances vouchsafed vnto us; (for I must intreat you to giue me leave to joyne danger and deliuerance together, for the better stirring of you up to your dvtie. And then I doubt not but all of vs shall have cause to confesse before the Lord his louing-kindnesse and his wonderfull workes before the sonnes of men.

"And, first, to touch the danger of your people both in their passage to Virginia and after their landing there, may I not say, in the words of Job, 'Will yee giue the words of him that is afflicted to the winde?' As if he had said, when affliction itselfe, and the inmost sorrowes of my heart tell my tale, will you regard it? O! that your soules were in my soule's stead, that you felt as much sorrow as I doe. *Loquor in angustia mea, queror in amaritu animæ meæ,* I speake that that I speake from a world of trouble, I make my complaint in the bitternesse of my soule.

Surely, if some hundreds of those that miscarried in the infancie, and at the first beginning of your Plantation (which is exceedingly bettered in these two yeeres), were now aliue, I thinke they would speake no otherwise than Job spake : Wil you giue the words of thē that are afflicted to the winde ? Will ye not beleeue in what danger we were when some of vs made shipwracke vpon the supposed inchanted Ilands; when others of vs encountred with bloudie enemies in the West Indies ; when many of us dyed by the way; and when those that were left aliue, some perished ashore for want of comfortable prouisions and looking vnto, and others were killed with the bowes and arrowes of the savages, vpon our first landing there ? I presume I speake to melting hearts of flesh, as tenderly sensible of your brethren's woe, as heartily thankful for your owne good.

" And now, Beloved, since the case is altered, that all difficulties are swallowed vp. And seeing first, there is no danger by the way; neither through encountring of enemy or pyrate ; nor meeting with rockes, or sholes (all which to sea-faring men are very dangerous, and from all which your ships and people are farre remoued, by reason of their faire and safe passage through the maine Ocean); nor through the tediousnesse of the passage, the fittest season of the yeare for a speedie passage being now farre better knowne than before, and by that meanes the passage

itselfe made almost in so many weekes as formerly it
was wont to be made in moneths, which I conceiue to
be through the blessing of God, the maine cause of the
safe arriual of your last fleete of nine sayle of ships
that not one (but one, in whose roome there was
another borne) of eight hundred, which were transported out of England and Ireland[1] for your Plantation, should miscarry by the way; whereas, in your
former voyages, scarce 80 of a 100 arrived safely in
Virginia.

" And, secondly, seeing there is no danger after
their landing, either through warres, or famine, or
want of conuenient lodging and looking to, through
which many miscarried heretofore, for, blessed be
God, there hath beene a long time, and still is, a
happie league of peace and amitie, soundly concluded
and faithfully kept, betweene the English and the
Natiues, that the fear of killing each other is now
vanished away. Besides, there is now in your Plantation plentie of good and wholesome provisions, for

---

[1] Ireland has always been a hive from which America has
derived sturdy hewers of wood, to subdue the forests. On April
12, 1621, William Newce, of County Cork, offered to transport
two thousand persons to Virginia. Soon after Daniel Gookin, of
County Cork, brother of Sir Vincent Gookin, transported cows
and goats from Ireland. Newce and Gookin both settled in
Virginia. The former died a few days after his arrival; the
latter was living at Newport News, at the time of the massacre
in Spring of 1622, and his descendants are now numerous.

the strength and comfort not onely of the Colony, but also of all such as after their passage doe land ashore. There is also conuenient lodging and carefull attendance prouided for them till they can prouide for themselues, and a faire Inne for receiuing and harbouring them in James Cittie, to the setting up of which both your worshipfull Governour, Sir Francis Wyat, and your worthie Treasurer, Master George Sands,[1] doe write, that they doubt not but there will be raised betweene fifteene hundred and two thousand pounds, to which every man contributeth cheerfully and bountifully, they being all free-hearted and open-handed to all publique, good workes.   Seeing, I say,

[1] In 1621, Christopher Davison, second son of Sir William Davison, and brother of the poets, Walter and Francis, was elected Secretary, and George Sandys, brother of the President of the London Company, was elected Treasurer.   Before he left England he published a translation of five books of Ovid, to which Drayton alluded in a rhyming letter :—

> "And worthy George, by industry and use,
> Let's see what lines Virginia will produce ;
> Go on with Ovid, as you have begun
> With the first five books : let y'r numbers run
> Glib as the former, so shall it live long,
> And do much honor to the English tongue.

While in America, he translated the remaining books, and the whole was published in folio, with illustrations, in 1626, at London.   A sixth and pocket edition appeared in 1669.   He lived to be an old man, and died at the house of his niece, the widow of Governor Wyatt.   In the Register of Bexley Abbey is this entry :—"Georgius Sandys, Poetarum Anglorum sui sœculi facile princeps, sepultus fuit Martii 7 stilo Anglic.   An. Dom. 1643."

that now all former difficulties (which much hindered the progresse of your noble Plantation) are remoued, and, in a manner, ouercome : And that your people in your colony (through God's mercy) were all in good health, euery one busied in their vocations, as bees in their hiues, at the setting saile of your ship, the ' Concord,' from Virginia, in March last, O what miracles are these ? O what cause haue you and they to confesse before the Lord his louing-kindnesse, and his wonderfull workes before the sonnes of men !

" But, to passe from the danger and deliuerance of your people, who indangered, yea, lost their liues in setting up your Plantation, consider, I beseech you, *in the second place,* the danger wherein your colony stood at the time of Sir Thomas Gates arriving in Virginia from the Summer Ilands,[1] when it was concluded a few dayes after his landing, by himself, Sir George Summers, Captaine Newport, and the whole Counsell, by the general approbation of all, to abandon the Colony (because of the want of provisions), and to make for New-found-land, and so for England. And will not the hopefull setling of your Colony there, now under the government of a worthy and worshipfull Commander,[2] and a wise and wel-experienced Coun-

---

[1] Arrived May 21, 1610.

[2] Governor Francis Wyatt was the son of George Wyatt, who died in Ireland. He was nominated to the office by the Earl of Southampton. The MSS. Transactions of London Company

sell, stirre you up to confesse before the Lord his
louing-kindnesse, and his wonderfull workes before
the sonnes of men?

"But if neither the danger of your people, nor the
danger of your whole Colony abroad, and the deliuerance vouchsafed to them both be enough to stirre you
up to confesse before the Lord His louing-kindnesse;
then, I beseech you, *in the third place*, to consider the
danger of your own selues here at home, and what
masse of money have you buried in that Plantation?
How many of you had it not made to wish that you
had never put your hand to this plough? Nay, how
many of you had it not made to shrinke in your
shoulders; and to sinke (as it were) vnder the burden,

state:—"His Lordship proposed unto the Company a gentleman recommended unto him for his many good parts, namely,
Sir Francis Wyatt, who was well reputed of, both in respect of
his parentage, good education, integritie of life, and faire for-
tunes, being his father's eldest sonne, as also for his sufficiency
otherwise, being euery way, without exception, fittinge for this
place." In 1626 Wyatt returned to England. In 1639 he was
re-appointed Governor, but was soon succeeded by Berkeley.
He died in 1644, and was buried at Bexley, in Kent. His
mother was Eleanora, daughter of Sir John Finch; his wife
Margaret, the child of Samuel Sandys.

Chamberlain, in a letter to Sir Dudley Carleton, dated 19th
June 1623, writes:

"An unruly son of the Lady Finch's, whom she sent to
Virginia to be trained, within five or six days after his return,
fell into a quarrel with the watch, and was so hurt he died the
next morning."

and to be quite out of hope for euer seeing penny of that you had so largely depursed?

"And now, Beloued, is not the case altered? Are not your hopes great of seeing, nay, of feeling within a few years of double, treble, yea, I may say, of ten-fold for one?

"Do not all of you know what that religious and judicious overseer of your College lands there writeth unto you from thence?[1] 'No man,' sayeth he, 'can justly say that this country is not capable of all those good things that you in your wisedomes, with great charge, have projected, both for her wealth and honour, and also all other good things that the most opulent parts of Christendome do afford, neither are we hope-less that this country may also yield things of better value than any of those.'

"And surely, by that which I have heard and seene abroad in my travailing to India and Japan, I am confirmed in the truth of that which he doth write; for Japan, lying in the same latitude that Virginia doth—and if there be any ods, Virginia hath them, as lying more southerly than Japan doth—Japan, I say, lying under the same latitude that Virginia doth, aboundeth with all things for profit and pleasure, being one of the mightiest and opulentest Empires in the world, having in it many rich mines of gold and silver.

[1] George Thorpe's letter from James City, dated May 17, 1621.

" And had you not a taste of some marchantable commodities sent vnto you from Virginia some yeeres agoe, whilest that worshipfull and worthy Governour, Sir Thomas Dale, sent home vnto you samples of aboue a dossen seuerall good commodities from thence? Have you not now great hopes of abundance of corne, wine, oyle, lemmons, oranges, pomegranats, and all maner of fruites pleasant to the eye and wholesome for the belly ? And of plentie of silke, silke-grasse, cotton, wooll, flax, hemp, &c., for the backe ? Are you not already possessed with rich mines of copper and yron, and are not your hopes great of farre richer minerals ?

" Have you not read what of late your worthie Treasurer[1] doth write unto you? 'If' (sayth hee) 'we overcome this yeere the Iron-workes, Glasse-workes, Salt-workes ; take order for the plentifull setting of corne, restraine the quantitie of tobacco, and mend it in the qualitie, plant vines, mulberry trees, fig trees, pomegranats, potatoes, cotton-wooles ; and erect a faire Inne in James Citie (to the setting up of which I doubt not but wee shall raise fifteene hundred or two thousand pounds, for every man gives willingly towards this and other public works), you have enough for this yeere.'

" And a little after, in the same letter, ' Maister

---

[1] George Sandys' letter of March 3, 1621-2.

Pory[1] deserves good incouragement for his paineful discoveries to the southward, as far as the Choanoack, who, although he hath trod on a little good ground, hath past through great forests of pynes, 15 or 16 myle broad, and above 60 mile long, which will serve well for masts for shipping, and for pitch and tarr, when we shall come to extend our Plantation to those borders.

" ' On the other side of the river there is a fruitfull countrie, blessed with aboundance of corne, reaped

---

[1] John Pory was a graduate of Cambridge, a protegé of Hakluyt, a great traveller and good writer, but gained the reputation of being a chronic tippler, and literary vagabond and sponger. A letter-writer on August 11, 1612, says :—"It is long since I heard of Master Pory, but now at last understand he lies lieger at Paris, maintained by the Lord Carew."

Sir Dudley Carleton, wrote on July 9, 1613, from Venice : "Master Pory is come to Turin with purpose to see those parts, but wants *primum necessarium*, and hath, therefore, conjured me with these words—*by the kind and constant intelligence which passeth betwixt you and my best friends in England*—to send him fourteen doubloons, wherewith to disengage him, where he lies in pawn, not knowing how to go forward or backward. I have done more in respect of his friends than himself, for I hear he is fallen too much in love with the pot to be much esteemed, and have sent him what he wrote for by Matthew, the post."

A correspondent of Carleton wrote on August 1 of the same year :—"You had not need meet with many such poor moths as Master Pory, who must have both *meat* and *money*, for *drink* he will find out himself, if it be *above ground*, or no deeper than the *cellar*."

In 1619, he was made Secretary of the Colony of Virginia, and after his recall (on account of his intolerable fees), while

twise a yeare; aboue which is the copper mines, by all of all places generally affirmed. Hee hath also met with a great deale of silke-grass, which grows there monethly, of which Maister Harriot hath affirmed in print, many yeeres ago, that it will make silke grow-graines, and of which and cotton wooll all the Cambaya and Bengala stuffes are made in the East Indies.'

"Heard you not with your own eares what Mr. John Martin, an Armenian by birth (that hath lived now six or seven yeeres in Virginia, and is but very

returning to England, he stopped at the infant Plymouth settlement, and had pleasant intercourse with Governor Bradford and William Brewster, with whom he may have been acquainted in Holland, and received from them some books, which he esteemed as "jewels," he says, in a note to Bradford, dated August 28, 1622, and signed, "Your unfeigned and firm friend." (See "Bradford's New Plymouth.")

A letter from London, dated July 26, 1623, says:—"Our old acquaintance, Mr. Pory, is in poor case, and in prison at the Terceras, whither he was driven by contrary winds, from the North coast of Virginia, where he had been upon some discovery, and upon his arrival, was arraigned and in danger to be hanged for a pirate."

On his arrival in London, he associated with the disaffected minority of the Virginia Company, who succeeded in arousing the prejudices of the King, so as to deprive them of the government of the Colony.

In 1624, he was one of a commission appointed by order of James to proceed to Virginia, and report upon its condition. At Jamestown he displayed a lack of honour in bribing Edward Sharpless, clerk of the council, to give him a copy of their proceedings, for which the perjured clerk was made by the Virginians to stand in the pillory and lose an ear.

lately come from thence, who also far preferre Virginia to England, to returne thither againe with this resolution there to live and die), said, in the audience of your whole Court, the 8th of this instant? I have travailed, said he, by land, over eighteen several kingdomes, and yet all of them, in my minde, come farr short of Virginia."[1]

In concluding the second head of the discourse, the deliverances from danger, he referred to an event which had been much talked of by the members of the Virginia Company.

" I will fear no evill, saith David, neither great nor small; for it is all one with God to deliver from the greater stormes as well as the lesser. Some difference there is, indeed, of *dangers*, and *deliverances* out of them, but it is only such as in books printed on large, and lesse letter and paper, the matter not varying at all. For example, when God brought some of the ships of your former fleetes to Virginia in safty, here God's providence was seen and felt priuately by some; and this was a deliuerance written, as it were, in *quarto*, on a lesser paper and letter. But now, when God brought all of your nine ships, and all your people in them, in safty and health to Virginia; yea, and

[1] Besides Martin, the Armenian, Molasco, a Persian, was a member of the Virginia Company.

that ship Tyger[1] of yours, which had fallen into the
hands of the Turkish men-of-war, through tempest and
contrary windes, she not being able to beare sayle,
and by that meanes driuen out of her course some
hundreds of miles; for otherwise, of itselfe, the passage
from *England to Virginia* is out of the walke of Turkes,
and cleere and safe from all pyrates who commonly
lurke neere ilands and headlands, and not in the
maine ocean. When this your Tyger had falne (by
reason of this storme, and some indiscretion of her
master and people, who, taking the Turkes to have
been Flemmings bound for Holland or England, bore
up the helme to speak with them; for they needed
not, if they had listed, to have come near the Turkes,
but have proceeded safely on their voyage,) into the
hands of those mercilesse Turkes, who had taken from
them most of their victuals, and all of their service-

---

[1] The ships "Warwick" and "Tiger" left the Thames about
the middle of September, 1621, and carried maids and young
women for wives. A MSS. letter from the London Company
says:—

"By this ship ['Warwick'] and pinnace called the 'Tiger'
we also send as many maids and young women as will make up
the number of fifty, with those twelve formerly sent in the 'Mar-
maduke,' which we hope shall be received with the same Christian piety and charity as they were sent from hence.
The adventurers for the charges disbursed in setting them forth,
which, coming to twelve pounds, they require one hundred and
fifty of the best leaf tobacco for each of them. . . . . Their
own good deserts, together with your favour and care, will, we
hope, marry them all unto honest and sufficient men."

able sayles, tackling, and anchors, and had not so much as left them an houre-glasse or compasse to steere their course, thereby utterly disabling them from going from them and proceeding on their voyage; when I say God had ransomed her out of their hands, as the prophet speaketh, by another sayle which they espyed, and brought her likewise safely to Virginia, with all her people, two English boys only excepted, for which the Turkes gaue them two others, a French youth, and an Irish, was not here the presence of God printed, as it were, in *Folio*, on Royall Crowne paper, and Capitall Letters ?"

The discourse ended by urging two steps for the welfare of Virginia. First, to send faithful and approved preachers, and not such as "offer themselves hand-over-head."[1] He did not wish them to encourage men like those who had pressed themselves upon the East India Company, one of whom is described in their minutes as a man "of straggling humor, can frame himself to all company, and delighteth in tobacco and wine."[2]

In the second place, he exhorted them to "send over skilfull and painefull tradesmen and husbandmen, to follow their trades and cultivate the ground. Our Countrey aboundeth with people; your Colony wanteth

---

[1] "Virginia's God be Thanked," p. 29.
[2] Cal. State Papers. East Indies.

them. You all know that there is nothing more
dangerous for the estate of commonwealths than when
the people doe increase to a greater number and multitude than may justly parallell with the largenesse of
the place and country in which they liue. For even
as bloud, though it be the best humour in the body,
yet if it abound in greater quantitie then the vessell
and state of the body will contayne and beare, doth
indanger the body, and oftentimes destroy it; so,
although the honour of a king be in the multitude of
people, as wise King Solomon speaketh, yet when this
multitude of people increaseth to ouer great a number,
the commonwealth stands subject to many perilous
inconveniences—as famine, pouerty, and sundry other
sorts of calamities.

"Thus, hauing falne into this point of exalting God
in the congregation of the people, and the assembly of
the elders, I haue here good occasion offered to mee to
blesse God for the *prudence* and *prouidence* of this
honourable Lord Maior, and the right worshipfull the
Aldermen, his brethren; who, seeing this Cittie to be
mightily increased, and fearing lest the ouerflowing
multitude of inhabitants should, like too much blood,
infect the whole Cittie with plague and pouertie, haue
therefore, deuised, in their great wisdomes, a remedy
for this malady—to wit: the transporting of their
ouerflowing multitude into Virginia, which was first
put in practise in the Maioraltie of that worthy and

famous Lord Maior, Sir George Bowles, who sent ouer a hundred persons, the halfe of this charge being borne by the Citie, the other half by the Honourable Virginia Company, which worthy course was afterwards followed by the right worshipfull Sir William Cockins, in whose Maioraltie were sent ouer a hundred more in the like manner. And now likewise the right Honourable the present Lord Maior and worshipfull the Aldermen, his brethren, intend to continue this course, that they may ease the Citie of a many that are ready to starue, and do starue dayly in our streetes.[1]

[1] William Cockaine was a distinguished merchant; sheriff in 1609; chief of the new company of merchant adventurers, which gave King James a great banquet on June 22, 1609, at his house, and there knighted. He died in 1626, and the distinguished poet and divine, John Donne, preached his funeral sermon.

In June 1621, the company wrote to the authorities in these words, relative to homeless boys and girls of London :—

"To the Right Honorable Sir William Cockaine, knight lord mayor of the city of London, and the right worthys the aldermen, his brethren, and the worthys the common council of the city :—

"The treasurer, council, and company of Virginia, assembled in their great and general court the 17th of November, 1619, have taken into consideration the continual great forwardness of this honourable city in advancing the plantation of Virginia, and particularly in furnishing out one hundred children this last year, which, by the goodness of God, have safely arrived (save such as died in the way), and are well pleased, we doubt not, for this benefit, for which, your bountiful assistance, we, in the name of the whole plantation, do yield unto you deserved thanks.

. . . . . . Right Worshipfull, ye are plentifull in other good workes, the maintaining of your hospitals, and other publike workes in this famous Cittie; preach your munificence through all the world, as the faith and óbedience of the Romans was published abroad among all.   O be rich in well-doing this way likewise, that it may be sayd of you, 'Many have done worthily for the plantation in Virginia, but the honourable Citty of London surmounteth them all.'   Your Cittie, as I sayd, aboundeth in people (and long may it doe

"And forasmuch as we have now resolved to send this next spring very large supplies for the strength and increasing of the colony, styled by the name of the London colony, and find that the sending of these children to be apprenticed hath been very grateful to the people, we pray your lordship and the rest, pursuit of your former so precious actions, to renew the like favours, and furnish us again with one hundred more for the next spring.

"Our desire is that we may have them of 12 years old and upward, with allowance of £3 apiece for their transportation, and 40s. apiece for their apparel, as was formerly granted. They shall be apprenticed; the boys till they come to 21 years of age; the girls till like age, or till they be married, and afterward they shall be placed as tenants upon the public lands, with best conditions, where they shall have houses with stock of corn and cattle to begin with, and afterward the moiety of all increase and profit whatsoever.

"And so we leave this motion to your honourable and grave consideration."

The following letter of Sir Edwin Sandys, to one of the King's secretaries, Sir Robert Naunton, shows that the children were not always willing to embark :—

"The city of London have appointed one hundred children·

so), the Plantation in Virginia is capable enough to receive them.   O, take course to ease your Cittie, and to prouide well for your people, by sending them ouer thither; that both they of that Colony there and they of your owne Cittie here may liue to bless your prudent and prouident gouernment ouer them.   For I have heard many of the painfullest labourers of your Cittie, euen with teares, bemoane the desolate estate of their poore wiues and children, who, though they rise early, taw and teare their flesh all the day long with hard labour, and goe late to bed, and feede almost all the

from the superfluous multitude to be transported to Virginia, there to be bound apprentices upon very beneficial conditions. They have also granted £500 for their passage and outfit. Some of the ill-disposed children, who, under severe masters in Virginia, may be brought to goodness, and of whom the city is specially desirous to be disburdened, declare their unwillingness to go. The city wanting authority to deliver, and the Virginia Company to transport these children against their will, desire higher authority to get over the difficulty." (Cal. State Papers, Colonial Series.)

Another paper will throw some light on the abuses in this business :—

" *Sir Edward Hext, Justice of the Peace of Somersetshire,*
to the Privy Council :
" Upon complaint that Owen Evans, messenger of the Chamber, had a pretended commission to press maidens to be sent to Virginia and the Bermudas, and received money thereby, he issued a warrant for his apprehension. Evans' undue proceedings bred such terror to the poor maidens that forty have fled from one parish to obscure places, and their parents do not know what has become of them."

week long vpon browne bread and cheese, yet are
scarce able to put bread in their mouthes at the weeke's
end, and cloathes on their backes at the yeare's end;
and all because worke is so hard to be come by, and
there be so many of the same trade, that they cannot
thriue one for another.

"Right Worshipfull, I beseech you, ponder (as I
know you doe) the forlorne estate of many of the best
members of your Citty, and helpe them, O helpe them,
out of their misery : what you bestow vppon them in
their transportation to Virginia they will repay it at
present with their prayers, and when they are able
with their purses; and God, in the meanewhile, will
plentifully reward your liberalitie this way, with His
blessing vpon your famous Citie, vpon your selues,
vpon your posteritie.

"And that I may bend my speech vnto all, seeing
so many of the Lord's Worthies haue done worthily
in this noble action; yea, and seeing that some of
them greatly rejoyce in this, that God hath inabled
them to helpe forward this glorious worke, both with
their prayers and with their purses, let it be your
greife and sorrow to be exempted from the company
of so many honourable minded men, and from this
noble Plantation, tending so highly to the advancement of the Gospell, and to the honouring of our drad
Soueraigne, by inlarging of his kingdomes, and adding
a fifth crowne unto his other foure : for ' En dat

Virginia quintam ' is the motto of the legal seale of Virginia.[1]

"And let mee in a word shut up all, vnto you all, that hath been spoken with that exhortation of the Apostle: My beloved brethren, be yee stedfast,

[1] On October 20, 1619, the Company appointed a Committee to meet at Sir Edwin Sandys', "to take a cote for Virginia, and agree upon the Seale." On the 15th of the next month the device was presented for inspection. When the seal was presented to King James, he looked at the reverse with the figure of St. George slaying the Dragon, with the motto, "Fas alium superare draconem," referring to the heathenism of the Indians, and ordered that the motto should not be used. The reverse was then altered, probably to that design which appears on the frontispiece of Smith's *History of Virginia*.

The face of the legal seal was an escutcheon, quartered with the arms of England, France, Scotland, and Ireland; crested with a maiden Queen, with flowing hair and eastern crown; supporters, two men in armour.

Spenser, Sir Walter Raleigh's friend, dedicated his *Fairy Queen* to Elizabeth, "Queen of England, France, Ireland, and Virginia." After James of Scotland became King of England, Virginia could be called, in compliment, the fifth kingdom.

vnmoueable, aboundant alwayes in the worke of the
Lord; for as much as you know that your labour is
not in vaine in the Lord."

London has at length received its reward for the
liberality shown in transportation of the destitute to
America. George Peabody,[1] the descendant of an
honest immigrant to North Virginia, died toward the
close of the year 1869, having given £500,000 to the
poor of that City. After a solemn service in Westminster Abbey, his embalmed body was carried in
honour by a British Man-of-War, escorted by another
bearing the American flag, to his native land, and after
landing, the remains of the plain American citizen
were followed to their resting-place in the quiet village
cemetery by Prince Arthur, the son of Her Majesty,
Victoria, Queen of the United Kingdom of Great
Britain and Ireland, with some of the highest in rank
of the Army and Navy, the distinguished in science
and letters, and most eminent of the public men of the
United States of America.

A few weeks after its delivery, the discourse was
published with the following title :—

---

[1] "2nd April, 1635, embarked on board the 'Planter,' of
London ; Nicholas Trarine, Master ; bound for New England,
bringing a certificate from the Minister of St. Alban's, County
Herts, and attested by the Justices of the Peace, Francis Peboddy,
aged 21 years, husbandman."—*Notes and Queries*, Feb. 12, 1870.

VIRGINIA'S GOD BE THANKED

OR

A SERMON OF

THANKSGIUING

FOR THE HAPPIE

successe of the affayres in

VIRGINIA this last

yeare

Preached by PATRICK COPLAND at
Bow-Church, in *Cheapside,* before the Honorable
VIRGINIA COMPANY, on Thursday, the 18
of *Aprill* 1622. And now published by
*the Commandement of the said hono-
rable* COMPANY.

Hereunto are adjoyned some Epistles,
written first in Latine (and now Englished) in
the East Indies by *Peter Pope,* an Indian youth,
borne in the Bay of Bengala, who was first taught
and converted by the said P. C. And after baptized by Master *John Wood,* Dr. in Divinitie
*in a famous Assembly, before the Right
Worshipfull, the East India Company,*
at S. *Denis* in Fan-Church Streete
in *London,* December 22,
1616

LONDON
Printed by J. D. for *William Sheffard* and John Bellamie,
and are to be sold at his shop at the two Grey-
hounds in Corne-hill, neere the Royall
Exchange. 1622.

Prefixed to the Sermon is the following epistle from Copland, occupying three pages of the original pamphlet, which, as far as possible, is here reproduced.

TO

THE RIGHT

NOBLE AND HO-

NORABLE EARLES, BARONS

And Lords; And to the right worshipfull
Knights, Merchants, and Gentlemen, Adventurers for the Plantation in VIRGINIA;
all happinesse, external, internall,
and eternall, in Christ Jesus our
blessed SAUIOUR.

AFTER I had discharged the charge laid upon me by your Honourable and Worshipfull Court, and was presently after sollicited by some of your Honourable Societie, to present to the eye, what I had deliuered to the eare.

Though at first I was indeed very vnwil-
ling, at their intreatie: yet, being commanded by your Honourable Court to
publish what before you had intreated
mee to Preach, and weighing well with
my selfe, that words spoken, are soone
come, soone gone; but that written
withall, they make a deeper impression;
for, by striking as well the Eye of the
Reader, as the Eare of the Hearer, they
peirce his heart the better, and saue his
soule the sooner. Hereupon that I might
testifie how much I honour your lawful
commandements, and withall, that I
might confirme with my Pen, that grace,
which it pleased God to worke by my
Voyce, I have now yeelded to all of your
Requests, making that common to all,
which then was imputed to your Honourable
Court, and loue to your Noble Plantation. For seeing many of your Noble
and worthy Company have spent a great
part of their painefully gained estates vpon this honourable Action, and reioyce

in nothing more than in this, that God hath giuen them a price . in their hand, and a heart to use it for the furthering of this glorious Worke; How could I, at so earnest intreatie refuse to aduenture this mite of mine, among so many worthie adventures of theirs? How could I (I say) refuse to make their publique *Bountie* and your publique Thanksgiuing, yet more publique?

If your Honours will be pleased to take in good part what now I impart; it may proue a spurre vnto me, to vndertake some better piece of seruice for the good of your noble Plantation; at least, if it lie in my poor power to bring it to passe. Thus intreating your Honours fauourable acceptance, I rest

In all humble dutie
to be commanded,

London, this 22 of   P. C.
   May, 1622.

CHAPTER IV.

THE effect of the Sermon in Bow Church was most happy. Increased interest in the welfare of the colony was manifested by the London people, and the Company resolved to push on the work of education with vigour.

In the month of June there sailed from England Leonard Hudson a carpenter, his wife, and five apprentices, for the purpose of erecting the East India school at Charles city.

The governor and council of Virginia were at the same time informed, that as the Company had failed to secure an usher, upon second consideration it was thought good to give the colony the choice of the schoolmaster or usher, if there was any suitable person for the office. If they could find no one, they were requested to inform them what they would contribute toward the support of a schoolmaster, and they would then again strive to provide "an honest and sufficient man." The letter concludes by saying, "there is very much in this business that we must leave to your care and wisdom, and the help and assistance of good people, of which we doubt not."

On July 3, 1622, the court gave order that a receipt should be sealed for £47 16s., which the gentleman mariners had given to the East India Company to be employed in laying the foundation of a church in Virginia.

The court thought fit to make Captain Martin Pring (the captain of the "Royal James") a freeman of the Company, and to give him two shares of land in regard of the large contribution which the gentlemen and mariners of that ship had given towards good works in Virginia, whereof he was an especial furtherer.

The placing and entertainment of Mr. Copland in Virginia being referred by the former court to the consideration of a committee, they having accordingly advised about it, did now make report of what they had done therein, as followeth, viz:—

1. First, they thought fit that he be made rector of the intended college in Virginia for the conversion of the infidels, and to have the pastoral charge of the college tenants about him.

2. In regard of his rectorship, to have the tenth part of the profits due to the college out of their lands and arising from the labours of their tenants.

3. In regard of his pastoral charge, to have a par-

sonage there erected, according to the general order for parsonages.

And for that it was now further moved that he might be admitted of the council, then it was referred to the former committee to consider thereof and of some other things propounded for his better accommodation there.

The committee appointed for the college for this present year are the ensuing, viz. :—Sir Edwin Sandys, Sir John Danvers, Mr. Gibbs, Mr. J. Ferrar, Mr. R. Smith, Mr. Wrote, Mr. Barbor.

The report of the committee touching Mr. Copland's placing and entertainment in Virginia was now read, they having thought fit he be made rector of the intended college there for the conversion of the infidels, and to have the pastoral charge of the college there for the conversion of the infidels, and to have the pastoral charge of the college tenants about him ; and in regard of his rectorship, to have the tenth part of the profits due to the college out of the lands and arising from the labours of their tenants; and in respect of his pastoral charge, to have a parsonage there erected according to the general order for parsonages which this court hath well approved of ; and have likewise admitted him to be one of the council of Virginia.

A few days after the election of Copland as Rector of the College, but before he could make arrangements

F

to leave, a tale of horror spread like wild-fire through the streets of London, the hearing of which made the "hair of the flesh to stand up," and froze the hearts of those who had been devising good things for Virginia.

A ship arrived from America with the horrible tidings, that at the very hour they were engaged in public thanksgiving for the happy league of peace with the Indians[1] at Bow Church, the Colony was a scene of desolation. The treacherous Indians on Good Friday had risen, and simultaneously attacked the several settlements, and killed nearly three hundred and fifty persons.

Among the mutilated bodies of the slain was that of the refined and educated gentleman, George Thorpe, who had the oversight of the college lands and tenants. After the Company received intelligence of his death, they made a particular request that George Sandys, the brother of Sir Edwin, a poet and translator of the Metamorphosis of Ovid, then Treasurer of the Colony, should take charge of the college interests;[2] and they wrote: "we esteem the college

---

[1] See page 57.

[2] In the dedication of the completed translation of Ovid to Charles the First, Sandys alludes to his residence as a Colonial Official in Virginia. He writes—"Your gracious acceptance of the first-fruit of my travels, when you were our hope, as now our happiness, hath actuated both will and power to the finishing of this piece: being limn'd by that unperfect light, which was

affairs not only a public but a sacred business." After this we know of but one allusion to the college. In 1623, Edward Downes petitioned " that his son Richard Downes, having continued in Virginia these four years, and being bred a scholar, went over in search of preferments in the college there, might now be free to live there of himself, and have fifty acres of land."

One year after the dissolution of the Virginia Company, in 1624, another attempt was made to erect the East India free school. Mr. Caroloff and others were sent over for the purpose, but he seems to have become unpopular. The governor and council, under date of June 15, 1625, write ·

" We should be ready with our utmost endeavours to assist the pious work of the East India free school, but we must not dissemble that, besides the unseasonable arrival, we thought the acts of Mr. Caroloff will

snatcht from the hours of the night and repose; for the day was not mine, but dedicated to the service of your great father and your self; which, had it proved as fortunate, as faithful in me and others more worthy, we had hoped, ere many years had turned about, to have presented you with a rich and well-peopled kingdom, from whence now, with myself, I only bring this composure: 'Inter victrices hederam tibi serpere laurus.' It needeth more than a single denization, being a double stranger, sprung from the stocke of the ancient Romans, but *bred in the New World,* of *the rudeness whereof it cannot but participate; especially having wars and tumults to bring it to light,* instead of the Muses."

overbalance all his other sufficiency though exceeding good."

A year before Copland made the collection on board of the "Royal James" for the benefit of Virginia, a company of English Non-conformists that had been residing at Leyden landed on the Atlantic coast, several degrees north of Jamestown, and commenced a settlement called New Plymouth. From that time there were two distinct waves of immigration, the educated and religious preferring the Northern, because King James had made the Southern a penal colony.[1] Early in 1620 the first large instalment of vagabonds and destitute persons arrived in Virginia, and yearly their numbers increased, and the desire for schools and churches proportionally decreased.

The social position of the settlers in the northern Colony had been far superior. Humphrey, the first Deputy-Governor of Massachusetts, was the son-in-law of the amiable and cultivated Countess of Lincoln, and another of her daughters, Lady Arbella, had married one of the settlers at Salem.

---

[1] Wroth published the same year the following lines in his *Abortive of an Idle Hour* :—

> "They say a new plantation is intended,
>   Neere or about the Amazonian river,
> But sure that mannish race is now quite ended.
>   O, that Great Jove, of all good gifts the giver,
> Would move King James, once more, to store that clyme
> With the moll cut-purses of our bad time."

Although the project of Henrico College in Virginia was not carried out, an institution of learning was planted at Cambridge, in New England, called Harvard, after a clergyman, who was one of its earliest benefactors. It soon began to graduate scholars, and upon the restoration of monarchy in England, one of its alumni became a chaplain of Charles the Second. At this period, too, there were thirty or forty graduates of Oxford and Cambridge in the pulpits of Massachusetts and Connecticut, and not more than three or four educated clergymen in Virginia. The year after the accession of Charles the Second a pamphlet was written by a clergyman who had lived in Virginia, and dedicated to the Bishop of London, in which he states that schools there were so few that " there was a very numerous generation of Christian children born in Virginia unserviceable for any employment of Church or State," and also adds that the members of the House of Burgesses were "*usually such as went over servants thither;* and though by time and industry they may have obtained competent estates, yet, by reason of their poor and mean condition, were unskilful in judging of a good estate either of Church or Commonwealth, or of the means of procuring it."[1]

Generation after generation the illiterate and unruly continued to be transported to Virginia, until, as the

[1] Records show that Edinburgh used to banish the nightwalking women to Virginia.

accurate Stith, the first historian of that commonwealth, admits, that it was disgraced in the eyes of the world, corroborating the strong language used by Sir Josiah Child, in his *New Discourse of Trade*, published in 1698:

" Virginia and Barbadoes were first peopled by a sort of loose, vagrate people, vicious, and destitute of means at home, being either unfit for labour, or such as could find none to employ themselves about, or had so misbehaved themselves by whoreing, thieving, and debauchery, that none would give them work, which Merchants and Masters of Ships, by their Agents or Spirits, as they were called, gathered up about the streets of London, and other places, to be employed upon Plantations."[1]

More than sixty years after the establishment of Harvard University, near Boston, the project of a

---

[1] As the descendants of these people increased in wealth they grew ashamed of their fathers, and became manufacturers, not of useful wares, but of spurious pedigrees. A letter written by a native of Virginia, a century ago, alludes to the assumptions of the planters of Virginia and Jamaica in these words:

" It really seems to me, much as I have heard in Virginia upon the subject of old families, that of all vanity it is the most extravagant. . . . To such an extent is this upstart feeling carried in Jamaica, that the favourite study is heraldry and genealogy. Many who have risen to wealth by cultivating coffee and distilling rum, have immediately turned their backs upon those interesting and useful articles, and employed them-

college for Virginia was revived. In the year 1683 the sum of £20 was paid out of the secret service fund of the King for the transportation of James Blair as chaplain to Virginia. He was a native of Scotland, a country which, a hundred years before, had enacted, in solemn assembly, that there should be a school in every parish, for the instruction of youth in grammar, the Latin language, and the principles of religion; and at a later period, that the school should be so far supported by the public funds as to render education accessible to even the poorest in the community. Macaulay, in his *History of England*, referring to the school law of Scotland, says the effect of its passage was immediately felt: " Before one generation passed away it began to be evident that the common people of Scotland were superior in intelligence to the common people of any other country in Europe. To whatever land the Scotchman might wander, to whatever calling

selves in manufacturing a pedigree. The ablest members of the College of Heraldry in London have been uniformly unable to send these forth, except with wanting links, bars sinister, and great gaps, rents and fissures, which reminds one of a book with pages here and there torn from it. Still they pride themselves on this ' open-work' style of genealogy, have these fancy documents recorded, with their arms wholly invented, and at the end of fifty years assume what they suppose to be the air of patricians. While genuine aristocrats hold them in contempt, the middle classes treat with bitter ridicule their spurious reputations."—" *Adventures of my Grandfather.*" By J. R. Peyton. London, 1867.

he might betake himself, in America or India, in trade or in war, by the advantage which he derived from his early training, he was raised above his competitors."

A graduate of the University of Edinburgh in 1673, and gifted with the "*fervidam vim Scotorum,*" he began to agitate anew the scheme of a college, which which had been so dear to Copland. The project met with opposition from the masses, who were too ignorant to appreciate its advantages, and from Sir Edmund Andros; but Blair did not shrink from a good fight, and at last obtained a charter for the College of William and Mary, at Williamsburgh. The preamble to the Statutes of the College gives the following sad account of the illiterate condition of Virginia at the commencement of the eighteenth century :—[1]

---

[1] It is a great relief to the true but dark picture of the ignorant condition of the first families in Virginia, to consider the high degree of intelligence that now prevails in America.

The *godless* system of Public Instruction, as its opponents in America term it, has produced the following fruits :—

The report prepared by Prof. Henry B. Smith, D.D., in behalf of the American Branch, for the Fifth General Conference of the Evangelical Alliance, held in Amsterdam, furnishes a mass of valuable information, from which we glean the following facts :—

Three-fourths of the entire population are under the dominant influence of the chief Protestant Churches; and the largest development and increase of Christianity in this century has been found in the United States. The Methodists have increased in the number of their communicants from 15,000 to over

" Nowhere was there any greater danger on account of ignorance and want of instruction than in the English colonies of America, in which the first planters had much to do in a country overrun with weeds and briers, and for many years infested with the incursions of the barbarous Indians, to earn a mean livelihood with hard labour. There were no schools to be found in those days, nor any opportunity for good education.

"Some few, and a very few, indeed, of the richer sort, sent their children to England to be educated, and there, after many dangers from the seas and enemies, and unusual distempers occasioned by the change of country and climate, they were often taken off by small-pox and other diseases. *It was no wonder*

2,000,000; the Baptists from 35,000 to nearly 1,700,000; the Presbyterians from 40,000 to 700,000; the Congregationalists from 75,000 to 275,000; the Lutherans number over 300,000 communicants; the Episcopalians over 160,000; and the German Reformed more than 100,000. Each of these churches reaches a population about four times as large as the number of its church members.

The increase of church-membership has relatively outrun the increase of population, and this in spite of the growing influx of foreign and largely papal population. In 1800, the total population was 5,305,935; and the church members numbered 350,000: in 1860, the total population was 31,443,321; church members, 5,035,250. Thus the ratio in 1800 was one communicant to about fifteen of the population; in 1832, it was one to ten; and in 1860, one to six.

The church edifices in this country in 1860 numbered 54,000, of the value of $171,390,432; and the number had increased 50 per cent. during the previous ten years. The Methodists had

if this occasioned a great defect of understanding and all sort of literature, and that it was followed with a new generation of men far short of their forefathers, which, if they had the good fortune, though at a very indifferent rate, to read and write, had no further commerce with the muses or learned sciences, but spent their life ignobly with the hoe and spade, and other employments of an uncultivated and unpolished country. There remained still, notwithstanding, a small remnant of men of better spirit, who had the benefit of better education themselves in their mother country, or at least had heard of it from others. These men's private conferences among themselves produced at last a scheme of a free school and college."

The Virginia Company, on account of its popular

19,883, averaging $2,000 each; the Baptists, 11,211, at $1,700 each; the Presbyterians and Congregationalists, 8,953, at $5,500 each; the Romanists, 3,795, etc.

The aggregate receipts of twenty-five missionary and philanthropic associations one year before and one year after the war, were about $2,250,000 in 1860, and over $5,000,000 in 1866. And the total amount given in large sums during the four years ending with 1866, to colleges, seminaries, and schools of high grade cannot have been less than seven or eight millions of dollars: thus illustrating the safety of relying on the voluntary principle, even amid the distresses and sacrifices of war.

The land grants in aid of Education by the United States of America have been—

For Common Schools, ...Acres—		67,983,914
,, Universities, ... ,,		1,082,880
,, Agricultural and Scientific Schools,.. ,,		9,510,000

sympathies, was looked upon by King James as the nursery of a seditious Parliament. After its charter was revoked, the £300 which had been bequeathed for the educating of Indian children, was transferred to the Bermudas, or Somers Islands Company, an outgrowth of the Virginia Company. Copland then proceeded to Bermudas, as a planter of Christian civilization, and laboured there for many years. His friend, Nicholas Ferrar, jr., of a retiring and contemplative disposition, forsook the marts of busy London, and receiving ordination in the Church of England, retired with his aged mother, to Little Gidding, where with nieces and nephews, he passed his days in doing good, and his nights in holy vigils, inclined to adopt the ritualism of Laud, yet sincere, self-denying, zealous in good works, and beloved by the sweet poet, George Herbert, and other intimate friends.

Copland, on an isle of the sea, as suitable for contemplation as Patmos, inclined to the simplest forms of worship consistent with propriety, efficacy, and solemnity, and there became convinced that the State should never interfere with any religious worship that did not disturb its peace, nor retard the prosperity of the commonwealth.[1] On the 27th of October, 1645,

---

[1] Norwood, who came to Bermudas in 1615, as Surveyor and Schoolmaster, in 1642, aged 71 years, wrote to William Prynne, protesting against the new church organization to which Copland and others belonged. From his letters, published in 1646, in

the House of Commons, upon the petition of those in
Bermudas, "Ordered, that the inhabitants of the
Summer Islands, and such others as shall join themselves to them, shall, without any molestation or
trouble, have and enjoy the liberty of the conscience
in matters of God's worship, as well in those parts of
Amiraca where they are now planted, as in all other
parts of Amiraca, where hereafter they may plant."

Copland, with his wife and others, about this
period, left Bermudas, and went to a small isle of the
Bahamas group, to form a church which should have
no connection with the State, and the Puritans on the
James River, in Virginia, were invited to seek the
same spot, which, in view of the entire freedom of
worship, was called Eleuthera. The Virginia Non-
conformists declined the proposition, but soon after
moved to the vicinity of Annapolis, on the shores of
the Chesapeake, and by their influence that Province
passed the "Act of Religious Toleration," which gave
Maryland a favourable reputation throughout the
civilized world.[1]

Prynne's *Blazing Stars*, it is learned that the new Church observed
a weekly love-feast, rejected infant baptism, and used a catechism
prepared by Oxensteirn, called "Milk for Babes." The officers
were—*Pastor*, Rev. N. White, formerly of Knightsbridge, near
Westminster; *Elders*, Rev. Mr. Golding, a young man, and Rev.
P. Copland; *Deacon*, Robert Cesteven, Esq., Councillor.

[1] Blome, in his *Britannia*, published in 1673, to which work
Lord Baltimore was a subscriber, says, the Assembly of Maryland
advised him to proclaim the Act of Toleration. See page 329.

The isle upon which Copland and his associates landed proved a dreary place, and the friends of religion in Boston, Massachusetts, were obliged to send them supplies, and in 1651 many of them returned to Bermudas, where Copland, then more than fourscore years of age, must have soon died.

Eleuthera still remains on the maps as the name of the small isle of the sea, but it is of no more worldly importance than Nazareth, in Galilee. The principles advocated there have, however, lived and spread, and the United States of America has become an Eleuthera, the land of civil and religious freedom, where each State instructs its youth in morality and such knowledge as will make them industrious, and thus diminish vice and pauperism, but devolves upon the Church and parents the delicate responsibility of preparing them for the kingdom which is not of this world.